SPORTS GREATS
TOP 10
WORST INJURIES

DAVID ARETHA

IN FOOTBALL

Published in 2017 by Enslow Publishing, LLC.
101 W. 23rd Street, Suite 240, New York, NY 10011

Library of Congress Cataloging-in-Publication Data

Names: Aretha, David, author.
Title: Top 10 worst injuries in football / David Aretha.
Other titles: Top ten worst injuries in football
Description: New York : Enslow Publishing, 2017. | Series: Sports Greats | Includes bibliographical references and index.
Identifiers: LCCN 2016032455| ISBN 9780766083028 (Library Bound) | ISBN 9780766083011 (6 Pack) | ISBN 9780766083004 (Paperback)
Subjects: LCSH: Football injuries—United States—Juvenile literature. | Brain—Concussion—United States—Juvenile literature. | Sports—Physiological aspects—Juvenile literature.
Classification: LCC RC1220.F6 A74 2017 | DDC 617.1/02763326—dc23
LC record available at https://lccn.loc.gov/2016032455

Printed in China

To Our Readers: We have done our best to make sure all website addresses in this book were active and appropriate when we went to press. However, the author and the publisher have no control over and assume no liability for the material available on those websites or on any websites they may link to. Any comments or suggestions can be sent by e-mail to customerservice@enslow.com.

Photos Credits: Cover, p. 1 Louis A. Raynor/The LIFE Images Collection/Getty Images; pp. 4–5 Scott Halleran/Getty Images Sport/Getty Images; pp. 9, 11, 12 Bettmann/Getty Images; pp. 15, 17 Nate Fine/Getty Images Sport/Getty Images; p. 19 AP Photo/Paul Spinelli; p. 21 Brent N. Clarke/Getty Images Entertainment/Getty Images; p. 23 Focus on Sport/Getty Images Sport/Getty Images; p. 25 Al Pereira/Getty Images Sport/Getty Images; pp. 27, 39 John Biever/Sports Illustrated/Getty Images; p. 28 TOM MIHALEK/AFP/Getty Images; p. 31 Tony Tomsic/Getty Images Sport/Getty Images; p. 33 George Gojkovich/Getty Images Sport/Getty Images; p. 35 © AP Images; p. 37 Rick Stewart/Getty Images Sport/Getty Images; p. 41 Tom Dahlin/Getty Images Sport/Getty Images; p. 43 Jim Davis/The Boston Globe via Getty Images; p. 45 Kent C. Horner/Getty Images Sport/Getty Images; design elements throughout book: maodoltee/Shutterstock.com (football field), RTimages/Shutterstock.com (grass), EsraKeskinSenay/Shutterstock.com (football stadium), Prixel Creative/Shutterstock.com (football play).

CONTENTS

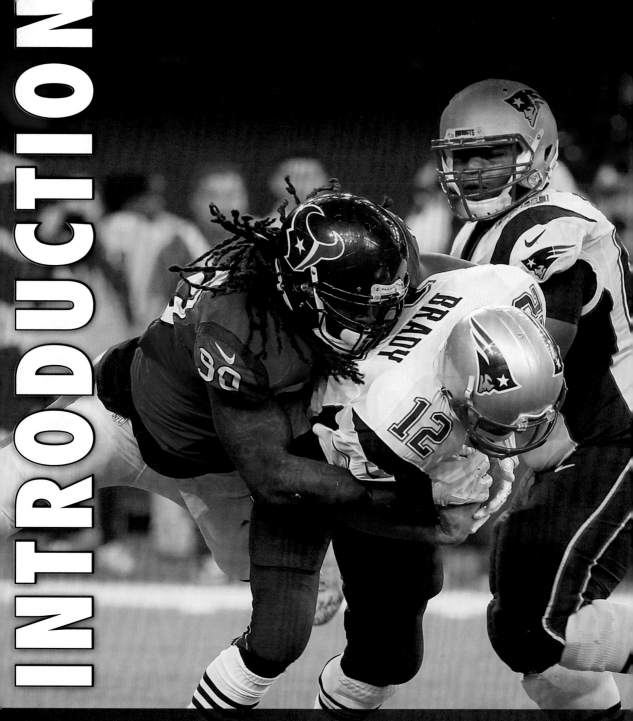

INTRODUCTION

New England Patriots quarterback Tom Brady feels the trucklike impact of a Jadeveon Clowney hit.

Y ou're an NFL quarterback, dropping back to pass. Suddenly, Jadeveon Clowney of the Houston Texans is charging toward you. The 6-foot-6 (1.9 meter), 270-pounder (122 kilograms) runs the 40-yard dash in 4.53 seconds. He's a Mack truck with a turbo-charged engine. When he hits, your bones, muscles, and organs jolt to one side. Pain shoots through your body. You feel a second blow when you slam to the ground. Hopefully Clowney doesn't fall on you. Hopefully you can get up. Hopefully your head didn't slam to the ground.

Football equipment has become more protective over the years, but the pads and helmet can protect only so much. All the while, players have gotten bigger, faster, and stronger. A big behemoth falling on you is bad enough. But when he's running at full speed, the impact is far greater. According to physics professor Timothy Gay, a 200-pound (90-kg) cornerback with a 4.56-second 40-yard-dash speed can produce 1,600 pounds (725 kg) of tackling force. Clowney would produce much more than that.

"You got a guy moving at that speed, hitting somebody, more damage is going to be done," St. Louis Cardinals wide receiver Larry Fitzgerald told NFL.com. "That's just the way football is. It's a violent game."

In pro football, knee injuries are the most common. If a player tears his knee's anterior cruciate ligament (ACL), he could be sidelined for a year—or forever. In the NFL, the average length of a running back's career is just two and a half years. In recent decades, head injuries have become the biggest concern. While broken bones heal, an injured brain can get much worse over time. In 2015, NFL players suffered 271 concussions—damage to the brain due to a blow to the head. And you don't need to be knocked out to suffer a brain injury.

Researchers from Boston University and the US Department of Veterans Affairs studied the brains of 91 former NFL players. In 2015, they reported that 87 of the 91 suffered from some level of chronic traumatic encephalopathy (CTE). The symptoms don't generally begin until about a decade later. First, a sufferer experiences headaches and dizziness. That could progress to memory loss, poor judgment, and erratic behavior. Many sufferers act irrationally and violently, even to loved ones. It could progress into deafness, tremors, and suicidal thoughts. Dave Duerson, Terry Long, and Junior Seau are among the former NFL stars, and CTE sufferers, who killed themselves.

Steps have been taken to reduce injuries. It is a severe violation to hit a player in the head, especially on purpose. An NFL player who does so could be ejected from the game, fined, and suspended. Though we love watching football, we should always keep in mind the dangers that players face. The players in this book suffered some of the worst injuries in NFL history. Some lost their ability to walk, while others lost their lives.

DEATH ON THE FIELD
PLAYER: CHUCK HUGHES
TEAM: DETROIT LIONS
OPPONENT: CHICAGO BEARS
SETTING: DETROIT, OCTOBER 24, 1971

For nearly sixty years, a sense of doom and gloom has hovered over the Detroit Lions. They have won only one play-off game since 1957. But on October 24, 1971, the situation was far grimmer. Lions wide receiver Chuck Hughes died during the game. It remains the only on-field fatality in the history of the NFL.

"It was a raw and dreary Sunday," remembered Lions fan Richard Bak, who shivered in the stands at Tiger Stadium. "A steady, melancholic rain fell all afternoon."

The Lions, in the midst of a 7–6–1 season, trailed the Chicago Bears 28–23. It was late in the fourth quarter, but Detroit still had a chance—thanks to Hughes. With the Lions on their own 31-yard line, quarterback Greg Landry threw downfield to his 5-foot-11 (1.8-meter) wide receiver, who made a tumbling grab. For Hughes, the 32-yard reception was the highlight of the season—his only catch of the year.

Throughout the stadium, fans asked, "Who's Chuck Hughes?" Few knew that he had twelve, fourteen, or fifteen siblings (accounts vary). He hailed from Abilene, Texas, and he starred at Texas Western College. To this day, Hughes still holds records at the school, which is now the University of Texas-El Paso. In one game in 1965, he caught 10 passes for 349 yards, which set an NCAA record.

In 1967, the Philadelphia Eagles selected Hughes 99th overall in the NFL draft. He was a backup wide receiver and also contributed on special teams. He proved to be a wonderful teammate, always "patting people on the back and cheering them up," said Landry.

Hughes, twenty-eight years old, was the proud father of a twenty-three-month-old son, Brendon. Chuck's wife, Sharon, had been concerned about her husband's heart. He had reported chest pain, but the doctors at Henry Ford Hospital determined the condition was not serious. They were wrong.

After Hughes's exciting catch, Landry threw two incompletions. Now on third down, Hughes lined up to the right. A Bears cornerback stared into Hughes's eyes and noticed that they looked kind of strange. Hughes ran his play while Landry threw toward the goal line to tight end Charlie Sanders, who dropped the ball.

After the play, Hughes "turned around and headed for the huddle," Chicago defender Bob Jeter said after the game. "Then he just fell down."

After Hughes collapsed on the field, Chicago Bears linebacker Dick Butkus waved to the sidelines for help.

Lying on the wet grass, Hughes grabbed his chest. He began to spasm uncontrollably as medical personnel came to his aid. "It seemed so terribly long for anyone to get to him," Jeter said. Amid a dark sky and light rain, doctors and trainers tried mouth-to-mouth resuscitation and cardiac massage. It wasn't working. They placed Hughes on a stretcher and rushed him to Henry Ford Hospital. Roughly an hour after the game (won by Chicago), doctors pronounced him dead.

In the Detroit locker room, Sanders and kicker Errol Mann openly wept. Every one of his teammates would attend his funeral. Said Lions equipment manager Roy Macklem, "It made you realize how unimportant a silly football game is."

THE HIT THAT PARALYZED
PLAYER: DARRYL STINGLEY
TEAM: NEW ENGLAND PATRIOTS
OPPONENT: OAKLAND RAIDERS
SETTING: OAKLAND, AUGUST 12, 1978

D arryl Stingley's twenty-sixth year of life began so beautifully. On September 18, 1977, his birthday, he ran 34 yards for a touchdown and caught a 21-yard TD pass in a win over Kansas City. The young New England Patriots receiver had turned his life around. As a kid in Chicago, he had engaged in fighting and stealing. Yet he developed into an All-American wide receiver at Purdue University, and he now appeared to be a rising NFL star.

But before his year was over, tragedy struck. Stingley suffered the worst injury imaginable, one that left him a quadriplegic. It was perhaps the NFL's darkest day because the league was largely responsible.

During a 1978 preseason game, Stingley and the Patriots faced the Oakland Raiders, known as the hardest-hitting and nastiest team in the NFL. Safety Jack Tatum, famous for his bone-jarring hits, was nicknamed "the Assassin." Even in meaningless exhibition games, Tatum went all out.

On the infamous play, Stingley ran a simple route. He raced down the right sideline and cut across the middle. He leaped and stretched to reach Steve Grogan's pass, but it sailed out of his reach. As Stingley began his downward trajectory, Tatum charged toward him. It was like two cars hitting head on. Tatum rammed his helmet into the front of Stingley's helmet, and Stingley's head snapped backward. He fell to the ground.

The hit compressed Stingley's spinal cord and broke the fourth and fifth cervical vertebrae in his neck. He was left paralyzed, unable to move his arms and legs. He would never walk again.

"I was twenty-six years old at the time and I remember thinking, 'What's going to happen to me? If I live, what

Stingley is carted off the field after Oakland's Jack Tatum broke his neck with a ferocious hit.

am I going to be like?'" Stingley told the Associated Press a decade later. "And then there were all those whys, whys, whys. It was only after I stopped asking why that I was able to regroup and go on with my life."

Tatum was deeply troubled by the incident, but he never apologized. Technically, he had nothing

Former Patriots teammate Sam Hunt shares a smile with Stingley on September 4, 1979. The previous day, New England fans honored Stingley with a five-minute standing ovation before a game.

to apologize for. Back then, the NFL permitted helmet-to-helmet tackles. In fact, league officials realized that violent hits were an appealing aspect of their game—much like fighting in hockey.

"There wasn't anything at the time that was illegal about that play," Patriots head coach Chuck Fairbanks told ESPN.com. But, he added, "I do think probably that play was a forerunner for some of the changes in rules that exist today that are more protective of receivers, especially if there is head-to-head-type contact."

Stingley lived the rest of his life in a motorized wheelchair, which he was able to operate with his right hand. He did not give up on life. He wrote a book entitled *Happy to Be Alive* (1983), which revealed his uplifting sense of humor. Ten years later, he started a nonprofit foundation to help inner-city youth in Chicago.

Stingley and Tatum never spoke to each other after the tackle. In 1996, they were supposed to meet for a TV appearance. But when Stingley learned that the purpose of the show was to promote Tatum's book (*Final Confessions of NFL Assassin Jack Tatum*), he declined to participate.

On April 5, 2007, Darryl Stingley passed away. The medical examiner listed the causes of death as pneumonia, coronary atherosclerosis, quadriplegia, and spinal cord injury. He was fifty-five years old.

I n a 1991 episode of *The Simpsons*, Homer happily sits on his couch watching *Football's Greatest Injuries*. When he turns his head to listen to Marge, a cracking sound and then a cry of agony emit from his TV. "Oh great," Homer complains angrily to Marge. "You made me miss Joe Theismann!"

Theismann's broken leg in 1985 is probably the most famous injury in football history. Several reasons make it so. It happened to one of the game's most popular quarterbacks, and the tackler was linebacker Lawrence Taylor. The legendary L.T. was "reckless, magnificent...240 pounds of athletic fury," declared ESPN.com. The injury also occurred on ABC's *Monday Night Football*, meaning a huge audience witnessed Theismann's anguish.

Most importantly, the gruesome nature of the injury made it famous. Theismann's tibia (shinbone) cracked,

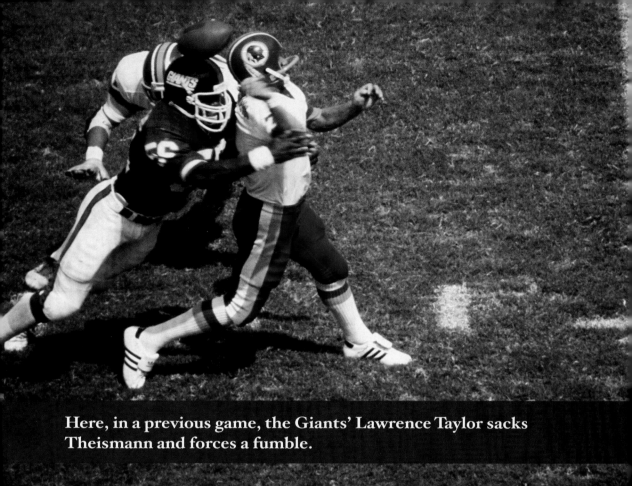

Here, in a previous game, the Giants' Lawrence Taylor sacks Theismann and forces a fumble.

with the popping sound reverberating throughout RFK Stadium. On replays, viewers could see the bone break through the skin. The film footage was so disturbing that Theismann couldn't watch it until twenty years later. "It made me sick...," Taylor said after the game. "It was the ugliest thing I'd ever seen."

Theismann had been in the public spotlight since the late 1960s, when he starred at the University of Notre Dame. His name originally was pronounced "Thees-mann," but those at the school changed the pronunciation to "Thighs-mann" because it rhymed with "Heisman." In 1970, Theismann finished second in voting for the Heisman Trophy, presented to college football's best player.

Handsome, talkative, and opinionated, Theismann played twelve years with Washington. He led the Redskins to the Super Bowl title during the 1982 season and earned First Team All-Pro honors in 1983. By 1985, he was dating Cathy Lee Crosby, a famous TV actor and show host. On November 18, he was on top of the world.

The infamous play occurred early in the second quarter of a scoreless game. It came on a trick play—a flea flicker. Theismann handed the ball to John Riggins. The burly running back ran toward the line, stopped, and pitched the ball back to his quarterback. As soon as he got the ball, Theismann was in trouble. Linebacker Harry Carson zeroed in on Theismann from the right, while Taylor freight-trained in from the left.

Taylor found himself behind Theismann and corralled him. At the same time, L.T.'s legs accidentally undercut Theismann's, causing the QB's right leg to twist sideways. The weight of Taylor and two other tacklers put hundreds of pounds of force on the shinbone, causing it to snap.

"Almost immediately, from the knee down, all the feeling was gone in my right leg," Theismann told the *Washington Post* in 2005. "The endorphins had kicked in, and I was not in pain. I remember looking up and seeing [head trainer] Bubba [Tyer] being on my left side. I looked at him and said, 'Please call my mom and tell her I'm OK.'"

But he certainly was not OK. During the ambulance ride to the hospital, Crosby tried to lift his spirits. "I joked that his punting game was finished," she told *People* magazine. So was his passing game. Theismann hoped to come back from the injury, but he never did.

Theismann later became a broadcaster for CBS, ESPN, and—ironically—ABC's *Monday Night Football*.

The Redskins' medical staff tends to Theismann's broken leg. Theismann said the break sounded like "two muzzled gunshots...pow, pow!"

As he lay on a stretcher in the Pontiac Silverdome, Mike Utley couldn't move. Fans feared that this injury was bad; in fact, it was one of the worst in NFL history. But as he was wheeled off the field, Utley gave fans a glimpse of his spirit: he flashed a thumbs-up, eliciting a lionlike roar from the emotional crowd. In the years that followed, the thumbs-up sign would be the symbol of the Mike Utley Foundation.

At 6-foot-6 (1.9 m) and ruggedly handsome, Utley had a zest for life. He captained the football and basketball teams at John F. Kennedy High School in Seattle. He earned First Team All-American honors as a guard for Washington State. And he helped the Lions surge to rare glory in his three years in the "Motor City."

The injury Utley suffered could have happened to anyone. On November 17, 1991, Utley attempted to block Los Angeles Rams defensive lineman David

Rocker. "I was focused. I was on my game," Utley recalled to SeattlePI.com. "I had my man the right way, doing what I needed to do." But in the heat of battle, Utley was shoved forward. Hard. His head hit the artificial turf with such force that he broke three vertebrae. He was left paralyzed from the chest down.

What appeared to be a tragedy has turned into a story of inspiration. On that same play, the Lions scored the go-ahead touchdown. They won that contest and their next six. Wearing "Thumbs Up for Mike" T-shirts, they advanced to the NFC Championship Game, their first appearance in thirty-four years.

More importantly, Utley proved remarkably resilient. Weeks after the injury, while still in Denver's Craig Hospital, Utley wanted to enjoy a beer while watching the Super Bowl. So he busted out of the place, wheeling himself four blocks

Ron Middleton and his Washington Redskins teammates honor Utley with the thumbs-up during the Super Bowl.

to a 7-Eleven. Once there, he asked the clerk to take the money out of his wallet. When he returned to his room, his hands and wrists weren't strong enough to open the can. But he persevered for an hour and a half, and eventually he cracked it open. He then watched his former Washington State teammate Mark Rypien lead the Washington Redskins to victory.

Since the injury, Utley has lived a rich life. In his home state, he shares a waterfront home with his wife, Dani. In 2008, SeattlePI.com reported that he worked out regularly at Gold's Gym and cruised the Columbia River in his 25-foot (7.6-m) boat. He has participated in archery, skiing (on a specially equipped chair), and even skydiving. One day, he and his wife shot at each other in mock warplanes while flying a mile above ground. "I love living," he explains.

In 1992, the Mike Utley Foundation was established. "We are dedicated to finding a cure and to provide motivational and emotional support for individuals who have been disabled with [spinal cord] injuries," states the foundation's website.

Years after the injury, Utley has been able to take small steps with the help of leg braces, crutches, or a walker. His ultimate goal is to "walk with [my] wife on the beach." With his determination, no one is betting against him.

Thumbs-up, Mike!

Utley was recognized at the 2016 Ellis Island Medals of Honor ceremony in New York City. His optimism and love of life are revealed in his smile.

HEAD-ON COLLISION
PLAYER: DENNIS BYRD
TEAM: NEW YORK JETS
OPPONENT: KANSAS CITY CHIEFS
SETTING: EAST RUTHERFORD, NJ, NOVEMBER 29, 1992

Coach Pete Carroll has won college national championships and a Super Bowl, but he has also witnessed the tragic side of football. On November 29, 1992, New York Jets defensive lineman Dennis Byrd slammed his helmet into a teammate, shattering a vertebra in his neck. He was rushed to the hospital, where doctors worried that he would never walk again. Carroll, the Jets' defensive coordinator at the time, drove to the hospital that night.

"When I got there...he started to get sick," Carroll told *Newsday*. "He was starting to throw up, which was frightening to the nurse, because you could literally suffocate....We had to all tip him over so he wouldn't choke on his own vomit. It was just horrible. Horrible."

Earlier that day—for a brief moment in time—Dennis Byrd had reason to celebrate. He stripped the ball from Kansas City quarterback Dave Krieg. But a millisecond later, tragedy struck. Immediately after the fumble, Byrd and teammate Scott Mersereau were about to make a Dave Krieg sandwich. Byrd, with his head low, charged toward the QB's right side. Mersereau zeroed

Byrd was a magnificent athlete before the injury, standing six-foot-five with a rock-hard 270-pound frame.

in on Krieg's left side. Krieg ducked forward, causing both defenders to miss the tackle. Instead, they crashed into each other. Byrd rammed the top of his helmet into Mersereau's chest, breaking his vertebra.

Jets teammate Kyle Clifton urged Byrd to get up. "I told him I had broken my neck and was paralyzed," Byrd told the *Oklahoman*. "The look on his face, I'll never forget that....He just looked like he was about to die."

Later that day, a Jets spokesperson said that Byrd was "paralyzed from the waist down and has no use of his legs and partial use of his arms." He added that it usually took two to three days to determine if such paralysis would be permanent.

As fans hoped and prayed for Byrd's recovery, they began to learn more about this 6-foot-5, 270-pound (1.9-meter, 122-kg) lineman. They read that he was kind, charitable, and churchgoing. He hailed from the small town of Mustang, Oklahoma, and had married his high school sweetheart. He and wife, Angela, had a toddler daughter, Ashtin. "I suppose I'm kind of a hopeless romantic," Byrd would tell the *Oklahoman*. "I like to watch sunsets, play with my kid."

Unlike other stories in this book, this one has a happy ending. After three months, Byrd began to walk again. Though he has yet to fully heal, he has been able to work on his ranch and raise four children.

In January 2011, Byrd even helped the Jets win a play-off game. Prior to that contest, against heavily

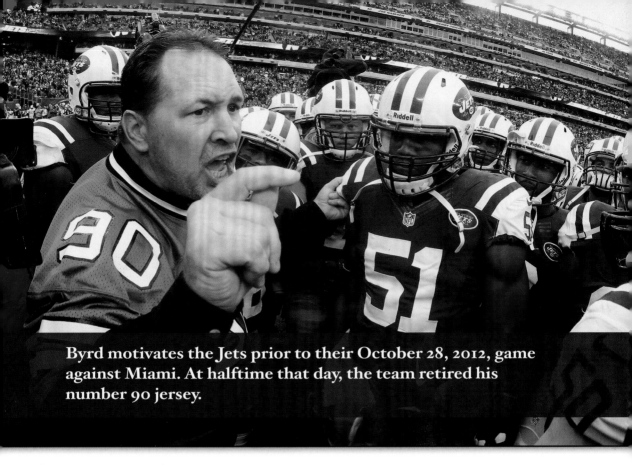

Byrd motivates the Jets prior to their October 28, 2012, game against Miami. At halftime that day, the team retired his number 90 jersey.

favored New England, Byrd motivated the Jets with a passionate speech. He recounted his injury and recovery, and he told them to "play like it's your last game. Give it your all." The Jets prevailed 28–21.

That night, Jets wide receiver Braylon Edwards tweeted, "I just heard the most inspirational message of my life from former Jet Dennis Byrd, who suffered a career-ending neck injury. As God [is] my witness, I have never been more ready to perform in my life. Dennis Byrd, I respect, salute, and honor you."

On October 28, 2012, the Jets honored Byrd by retiring his jersey number during a halftime ceremony. Byrd fought back tears as fans showered him with a standing ovation.

THE PLAYMAKER'S FINAL PLAY
PLAYER: MICHAEL IRVIN
TEAM: DALLAS COWBOYS
OPPONENT: PHILADELPHIA EAGLES
SETTING: PHILADELPHIA, OCTOBER 10, 1999

Philadelphia Eagles fans were the meanest in football. They threw snowballs at opponents. They booed Santa Claus. They often got into fights. In fact, in 1998 the team installed a court and a jail in Veterans Stadium because fans were so unruly.

A year later, Eagles fans hit a new low. They cheered while Michael Irvin was placed on a stretcher. The Dallas Cowboys wide receiver had suffered a head and neck injury. He couldn't move. He was temporarily paralyzed. And yet fans continued to applaud—not to express encouragement, but to show their happiness that he was hurt. "Putting him out of the game was probably the highlight of this season," an Eagles fan told the *Philadelphia Inquirer*.

Besides being mean, Eagles fans cheered for another reason. Michael Irvin was considered a show-off. He wore fur coats and flashy jewelry, and he performed fancy dances after touchdowns. His BMW's license plate said "PLY MKR," short for "the Playmaker."

They also disliked Irvin because they resented his and the Cowboys' success. In twelve years with Dallas, Irvin made the Pro Bowl five times and topped 1,000 receiving yards in a season seven times. The Cowboys won three Super Bowls during the 1990s and routinely finished ahead of the Eagles in the NFC East standings.

Irvin told the *Dallas Morning News* that it "was a compliment for Philly to cheer me." He said he knew what the fans were thinking: "Thank God he's leaving the field; he's been killing us...maybe now we have a chance to win."

Irvin flamboyantly celebrates a touchdown in the January 1993 Super Bowl against Buffalo. "The Playmaker" helped lead Dallas to three Super Bowl victories.

The brother of sixteen siblings, Michael Irvin had played and lived fearlessly—some say recklessly. After smashing records at the University of Miami, he was selected 11th overall in the 1998 NFL draft. With Dallas, he formed the "Triplets" along with two fellow

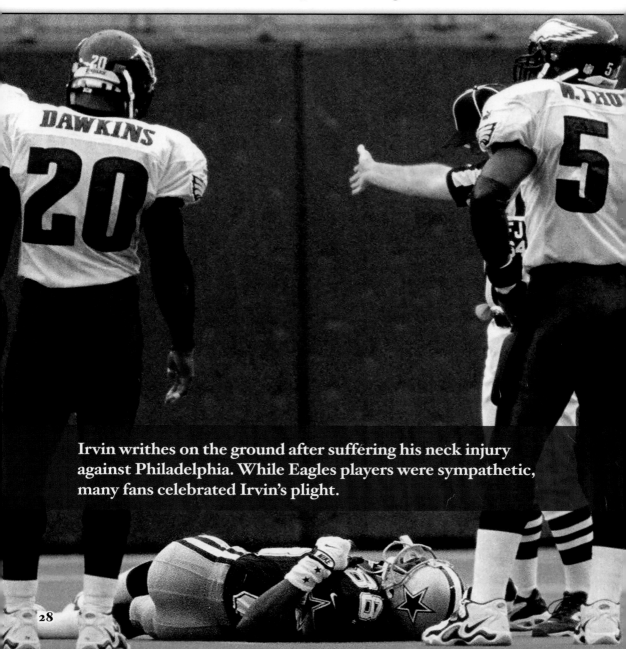

Irvin writhes on the ground after suffering his neck injury against Philadelphia. While Eagles players were sympathetic, many fans celebrated Irvin's plight.

superstars: Cowboys quarterback Troy Aikman and running back Emmitt Smith. Irvin ran crisp routes and outfought defensive backs for position. He courageously caught passes in the middle of the field, where receivers are vulnerable to bone-jarring hits.

Off the field, Irvin sometimes found himself in trouble. In 1996, he was convicted of cocaine possession. In 1998, he seriously cut a teammate with scissors during a playful fight. Despite all the risks he took, Irvin always returned to the field—until the infamous game against the Eagles.

In the first quarter, Irvin caught an Aikman pass and was immediately tackled by cornerback Bobby Taylor. The problem came when safety Tim Hauck came flying over to finish the play. With his helmet and shoulder pads, Hauck hit the back of Irvin's neck, jamming Irvin's head against the hard artificial turf. "I didn't think I hit him that hard," Hauck said. "It's part of the game, but when you see them doing all that work on him, all you can do is hope everything is all right."

Irvin was temporarily paralyzed due to swelling of the spinal cord. The swelling subsided, and he eventually regained full movement. However, he missed the rest of the season and was forced to retire.

Ten years later, Irvin was back on television, flashing his moves on *Dancing with the Stars*. No doubt, fans in Philadelphia were rooting against him.

Mike Webster was so tough, they called him "Iron Mike." When his Pittsburgh Steelers teammates bundled up during cold-weather games, he snapped the ball with bare arms. From 1974 to 1990, he played center in the NFL, butting heads with 300-pound (136-kg) linemen. He helped lead the Pittsburgh Steelers to four Super Bowl titles, and he made the Pro Bowl nine times. He gave his all...and his all was way too much.

By the time Webster retired, his body was a wreck and his brain was permanently damaged. He lived only twelve more years, much of which was spent in agony. He suffered from hearing loss and chronic pain to his back, knees, foot, shoulder, elbow, and hands—all of which had been injured or worn down on the football field. Most tragically, he suffered from chronic traumatic encephalopathy (CTE), a progressive degenerative disease of the brain.

Dr. Fred Jay Krieg, a clinical psychologist, told the *New York Times* that Webster was "the football version of punch drunk...It doesn't get better. You get more and more demented. It's sad."

Born in Tomahawk, Wisconsin, Webster built his muscles on a 640-acre (260-hectare) potato farm. He

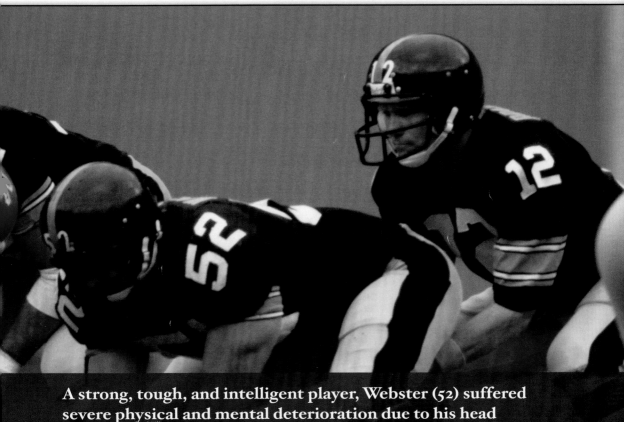

A strong, tough, and intelligent player, Webster (52) suffered severe physical and mental deterioration due to his head injuries. Here, he is ready to snap the ball to Terry Bradshaw.

starred at the University of Wisconsin before being drafted by the Steelers in 1974.

"I couldn't have been the player I was without him," said legendary Steelers quarterback Terry Bradshaw. "He was so smart, so prepared for everything we would face in a game. We all worked hard, but none as hard as Mike did."

After the 1988 season, the Steelers decided not to re-sign Iron Mike. He was thirty-six years old and all beaten up. He had played too much already. But the hyper-competitive Webster wanted more. The Kansas City Chiefs signed him as an offensive line coach, then allowed him to suit up at center for two years.

In retirement, Webster's head ached constantly. He took medications for pain, seizure prevention, depression, and anxiety. Doctors also prescribed Eldepryl, commonly taken by those who suffer from Parkinson's disease. Webster lived in such pain that he frequently Tasered himself. It was the "only way he could get to sleep," his son Garrett told ESPN.com.

Webster couldn't function or even think properly. He made bad investment decisions and lost huge sums of money. He and his wife, Pamela, parents of four children, divorced. He spent some nights sleeping in his truck. One night late in his life, Steelers fans saw him hunched over in a train station, munching on dry cereal.

Webster suffered so much head trauma that the frontal lobe of his brain was severely damaged. It caused cognitive dysfunction—an inability to think properly. He had trouble maintaining concentration. In his diary, Webster wrote dark, rambling entries. He developed terribly violent thoughts. He amassed weapons that he seriously considered using on NFL officials.

Webster was inducted into the Pro Football Hall of Fame in 1997, but his induction speech was uncomfortable to watch. He was forty-five years old but looked closer to sixty. He rambled with his words and couldn't maintain focus. Fans must have wondered: *Is this what the game does to its players?*

On September 24, 2002, Webster died of heart failure. "Unfortunately, he had some turmoil and misfortune after his football career," said former Steelers running back Franco Harris. "He is now at peace. We do miss and love Mike."

Here, in 1980, the twenty-eight-year-old Webster is already showing signs of age. He would die at age fifty.

HELMET TO HELMET

PLAYER: KEVIN EVERETT

TEAM: BUFFALO BILLS

OPPONENT: DENVER BRONCOS

SETTING: BUFFALO, SEPTEMBER 9, 2007

When Buffalo's Kevin Everett and Denver's Domenik Hixon banged helmets in the 2007 season opener, two careers were nearly ruined. Everett suffered a severe injury, one that doctors called life threatening a day later. For Hixon, the pain was emotional. He felt guilty about the injury and considered quitting football. Thankfully, for both men, this story has a happy ending.

When Everett took the field on September 9, 2007, few people knew his name. The Texas-born tight end had caught just one pass as a rookie in 2006; mostly, he played on special teams. After the frightening play in the second half, however, Everett was on everyone's mind.

The horrific collision occurred during the kickoff that began the third quarter. Hixon, a native of Germany, was playing in his first NFL game. He returned the kick to his own 20-yard line when Everett charged toward him. Everett lowered his head, preparing to plow into Hixon's chest. Not realizing Everett was coming, Hixon lowered *his* head, and the two warriors smashed helmets together. Hixon was OK, but Everett crumbled to the ground. He lay motionless on the field, moving only his eyes.

In an emergency surgery, Dr. Andrew Cappuccino repaired a fracture between the third and fourth vertebrae. He also inserted a plate and four screws in Everett's spinal column. Cappuccino gave his patient a "statistically very small" chance of walking again. Other issues, related to swelling and breathing, were "life threatening," the doctor said.

Everett lies on the field, unable to move, after banging helmets with Denver's Domenik Hixon.

Fortunately, Everett recovered remarkably well. By September 17, 2007, he had regained movement in both hands and gained strength in his legs. Everett and his family hoped he would be able to walk in a few weeks.

Meanwhile, Hixon struggled with guilt and sadness. "I was devastated," he told BuffaloBills.com in 2012. "It was one of those things that I talked to my parents about giving up football after that happened...I just felt so bad that I changed someone's life like that."

Hixon suffered nightmares, and his play got so bad that the Broncos released him after four games. The New York Giants soon signed him, and his meeting with Everett on December 23 changed his life.

Everett returned to Buffalo's Ralph Wilson Stadium that afternoon and walked in public for the first time. He also met Hixon and told him that the injury wasn't his fault—to not feel guilty. Hixon's outlook on life improved after that encounter. In the play-offs that year, his 290 kickoff return yards helped the Giants storm to the Super Bowl title.

Everett would never play football again, and he still deals with pain on a daily basis. According to a 2014 *Sports Illustrated* article, Everett wobbled a little when he walked and didn't have full sensation in his fingers. However, Everett has found new purposes in life. He started the Kevin Everett Foundation, which assists those with spinal cord injuries both financially and

Surgeon Andrew Cappuccino hugs Everett at halftime of a home game on September 7, 2008. That day, Everett received the George Halas Award, which honors an NFL member who overcomes adversity.

emotionally. And with his wife working as a teacher, he became a stay-at-home dad to his young children.

Like others who have stared death in the face, Everett appreciates the preciousness of life.

"It's just a beautiful thing," he said about his new role. "I love it. I enjoy every minute of it every day."

THE ULTIMATE COMEBACK
PLAYER: ADRIAN PETERSON
TEAM: MINNESOTA VIKINGS
OPPONENT: WASHINGTON REDSKINS
SETTING: WASHINGTON, DC, DECEMBER 24, 2011

Facing the Minnesota Vikings in 2012, the St. Louis Rams were desperate to stop Adrian Peterson. On a play in the second quarter, they put five men on the defensive line—almost unheard of in the NFL. But even that didn't work.

"Handoff, Adrian, up the middle," blared Vikings radio broadcaster Paul Allen. "Room. To the 20. Cuts to the left to the 25...and Adrian's *loose*! He splits the defense! Fifty! Forty! Thirty! Good-bye, baby! Touchdowwwwwn! That's an 82-yard touchdown by Adrian Peterson!"

In 2012, Peterson enjoyed "the greatest rushing season the NFL has ever seen," Allen said. Incredibly, it came a year after one of the worst injuries a running back could experience. Against Washington on Christmas Eve, 2011, Peterson plunged into the end zone on a 1-yard run. As he did, Redskins safety DeJon Gomes tackled him low, ramming his helmet against the side of Peterson's left knee. Adrian squirmed on the field, writhing in pain.

On Christmas Day, medical tests revealed devastating news: Peterson had torn the anterior cruciate ligament (ACL) and medial collateral ligament (MCL) in his left knee. "Torn ACL" is among the worst news a running back could hear. Years ago, such an injury would end a player's career. In modern times, players have been able to return to the field following surgery, but recovery time has been about a year. And that's just for the ACL. With the MCL also torn, "AP" faced an even

Showing no signs of his 2011 ACL/MCL injury, Peterson blasts downfield during a 2012 game against St. Louis. In this contest,

tougher comeback. Some journalists speculated that the twenty-six-year-old might have to retire.

But Adrian Peterson was no ordinary human being. Fast, powerful, and explosive, Peterson had made the Pro Bowl in each of his first four seasons (2007–2010). In 2008, he led the NFL in rushing with 1,760 yards. "It's not just his work ethic, it's his positivity," said teammate Toby Gerhart. "He's always at 100 miles per hour, pushing himself."

Peterson was determined to return for the 2012 season opener—just eight and a half months away. In fact, he said, "my ultimate goal is to come back 110 percent better than I was before." After healing from his surgery, AP began a ferocious rehabilitation effort. His routine included weight lifting, exercise machines, agility moves, pool therapy, and running up stadium steps—all the way to the top.

Peterson not only returned for the 2012 season opener, he was better than ever. He rushed for 84 yards and two touchdowns that day, and he improved as the season progressed. In November and December, he posted rushing games of 182, 171, 210, 154, 212, and 199 yards. He finished the season with 2,097 rushing yards, just nine shy of Eric Dickerson's NFL season record. The Vikings had a poor passing game, meaning defenses could focus on AP. Yet he still averaged 6.0 yards per carry.

Unfortunately, the Adrian Peterson story took a sad twist in 2014. He was convicted of recklessly assaulting his four-year-old son. As a form of punishment, he hit him multiple times with a tree branch—just like he himself had been punished as a child. In September, the NFL suspended him for the rest of the 2014 season. Peterson returned in 2015 and again led the league in rushing.

The NFL suspended Peterson for most of 2014, but he returned in 2015 (pictured). That year, he led the league in carries (327), rushing yards (1,485), and rushing touchdowns (11).

DEPTHS OF DESPAIR
PLAYER: JUNIOR SEAU
TEAMS: SAN DIEGO CHARGERS, MIAMI DOLPHINS, NEW ENGLAND PATRIOTS
DEATH: MAY 2, 2012

In 2010, Junior Seau fell asleep at the wheel of his SUV and plunged 100 feet (30 m) down a cliff. He sustained only minor injuries, but the incident served as a metaphor for his life. Seau rose from the lowest valley to the highest peak, then crashed into the depths of despair. All because of football.

The son of Samoan immigrants, Tiaina Seau Jr. grew up in San Diego, California. His family was so poor that Junior and his two brothers had to sleep in the family's one-car garage. "My two sisters, who lived inside the house, always bragged that they had a carpet in their bedroom," Junior told *Sports Illustrated*. "But we'd say, 'So what? We have the biggest door in the whole place.'"

Seau starred in football, basketball, and track in high school, then attended the University of Southern California (USC). Despite his stellar 3.6 grade-point average in high school, Junior scored only 690 on his SAT, making him ineligible to play as a USC freshman. But he persevered, and as a senior linebacker he recorded 19 sacks and was named First Team All-American.

In an NFL career that spanned twenty seasons, Seau became one of the greatest linebackers of all time. For the San Diego Chargers (1990–2002), he made twelve straight Pro Bowls and was named First Team All-Pro

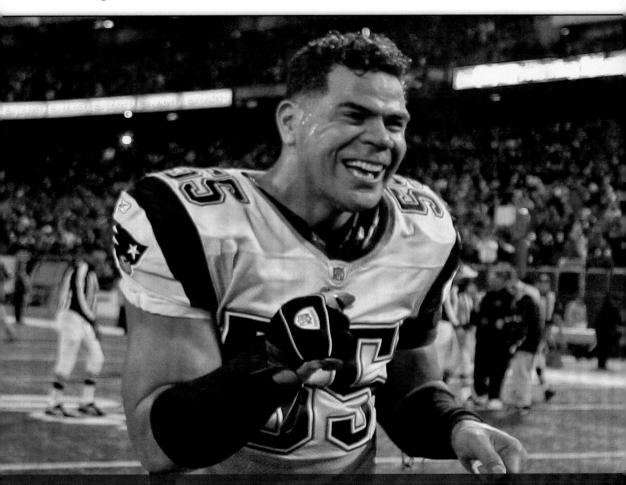

Seau displays his joy and passion for the game after a victory with New England. Sadly, his brain trauma changed his personality and made him suicidal.

eight times. He ran the 40-yard dash in a speedy 4.6 seconds, and he bench-pressed 500 pounds (226 kg). He also brought tremendous anticipation and leadership to the field. Coaches, teammates, and fans adored him.

"He was always so upbeat," Chargers general manager Bobby Beathard told ESPN.com. "He practiced the way he played. He made practice fun. He was a coach's dream. He was an amazing guy as well as a player and a person."

When Seau played, the NFL did not monitor head injuries like it does now. He had no *reported* concussions, but his wife, Gina , said that he did sustain concussions. "He always bounced back and kept on playing," she told ESPN.com. "He's a warrior."

In recent decades, we've learned that ignoring concussion signs is a bad idea. Damage to the brain can have serious long-term effects—as discussed in this book's introduction. Many former players who suffer from CTE lose their temper easily. A larger number abuse family members, and Seau himself was arrested for domestic violence hours before driving down the cliff.

Some people with CTE even become suicidal. On May 2, 2012, Seau himself took his own life. At his home in Oceanside, California, Seau shot himself in the chest. On a piece of paper, he had written the lyrics of his favorite country song, "Who I Ain't."

Fans mourned Junior's death and laid tributes in front of Seau's: The Restaurant in San Diego. Many consider him the most popular player in Chargers history.

I've tried to be the man I should, but sometimes I fall short.
I'm not a man of anger; I never meant to hurt no one.
But there are things in my life, I'm sad to say I've done.

After his death, Seau's family had his brain examined by doctors at the National Institutes of Health. They found clear evidence of brain trauma.

"I think it's important for everyone to know that Junior did indeed suffer from CTE," Gina Seau said. "It's important that we take steps to help these players. We certainly don't want to see anything like this happen again to any of our athletes."

GLOSSARY

All-American Athletes who are voted one of the best at each position, either at the high school level or the college level; many organizations announce All-American teams.

atherosclerosis The buildup of fats, cholesterol, and other substances in and on a person's artery walls.

cardiac massage A procedure to resuscitate a patient suffering from a heart attack; the rescuer rhythmically compresses the chest and heart to restore circulation.

cervical vertebrae The neck vertebrae in the spinal column.

concussion Damage to the brain caused by a blow to the head.

CTE Short for chronic traumatic encephalopathy; a progressive degenerative disease of the brain found in people with a history of repetitive brain trauma.

endorphins Chemicals in the brain that, when activated, raise a person's pain threshold.

melancholic In a state of gloom or sadness.

Pro Bowl The all-star game for NFL players, held after the season is over (played in Honolulu, Hawaii, since 1980).

quadriplegic A person who suffers from paralysis of all four limbs (inability to move them) or of the entire body below the neck.

SAT An exam intended to assess a student's readiness for college.

spinal cord Nerve fibers and tissue that are enclosed in the spine; connects most parts of the body to the brain.

vertebrae A series of bones that form a person's backbone (singular: vertebra).

FURTHER READING

Books

Basen, Ryan. *Injuries in Sports.* Edina, MN: ABDO Publishing, 2014.

Bryant, Howard. *The Best Legends, Games, and Teams in Football.* New York, NY: Philomel Books, 2015.

Editors of *Sports Illustrated for Kids. Football: Then to WOW!* New York, NY: Sports Illustrated, 2014.

Hudson, Maryann. *Concussions in Sports.* Edina, MN: ABDO Publishing, 2014.

Jacobs, Greg. *The Everything Kids' Football Book.* Fairfield, OH: Adams Media, 2014.

Nagelhout, Ryan. *What If I Get a Concussion?* New York, NY: Gareth Stevens Publishing, 2016.

Websites

NFL Rush

nflrush.com

Includes kids-oriented NFL stories, word games, quizzes, computer games, and tons of other fun stuff.

NFL Zone

sikids.com/nfl-zone

Sports Illustrated for Kids offers NFL stories that kids will enjoy, plus a "Cool Stuff" section, "Kid Reporter," and more.

Safe Kids Worldwide

safekids.org/preventing-sports-related-injuries

Includes articles, fact sheets, and checklists on how to stay as safe as possible while playing sports.

INDEX